Nita

HYDERABAD VEG

Nita Mehta

B.Sc. (Home Science), M.Sc. (Food and Nutrition)
Gold Medalist

© Copyright 2008 SNAB Excellence in Books Publishers Pvt Ltd

WORLD RIGHTS RESERVED. The contents—all recipes, photographs and drawings are original and copyrighted. No portion of this book shall be reproduced, stored in a retrieval system or transmitted by any means, electronic, mechanical, photocopying, recording or otherwise, without the written permission of the publishers.

While every precaution is taken in the preparation of this book, the publisher and the author assume no responsibility for errors or omissions. Neither is any liability assumed for damages resulting from the use of information contained herein.

TRADEMARKS ACKNOWLEDGED. Trademarks used, if any, are acknowledged as trademarks of their respective owners. These are used as reference only and no trademark infringement is intended upon.

First Edition 2008

ISBN 978-81-7869-271-5

Food Styling and Photography: SNAB Excellence in Books

Layout and Laser Typesetting :

Contributing Writers :
Anurag Mehta
Subhash Mehta

Editorial & Proofreading :
Rakesh
Ramesh

Distributed by :

THE VARIETY BOOK DEPOT
A.V.G. Bhavan, M 3 Con Circus,
New Delhi - 110 001
Tel : 23417175, 23412567; Fax : 23415335
Email: varietybookdepot@rediffmail.com

Published by :

SNAB Excellence in Books
Publishers Pvt. Ltd.
3A/3 Asaf Ali Road,
New Delhi - 110002
Tel: 23252948, 23250091
Telefax:91-11-23250091

Editorial and Marketing office:
E-159, Greater Kailash-II, N.Delhi-48
Fax: 91-11-29225218, 29229558
Tel: 91-11-29214011, 29218574
E-Mail: nitamehta@email.com

nitamehta@nitamehta.com
*Website:*http://www.nitamehta.com
Website: http://www.snabindia.com

Printed by :

CANARA TRADERS & PRINTERS PVT. LTD.,
CHENNAI.

Rs. 89/-

Introduction

Hyderabadi food has been popular worldwide and the exotic biryanis have found a place in almost every city of India. But now food-lovers need not look for an eatery for Hyderabadi food. This book provides the original recipes of the cuisine. From snacks to dessert, the best methods have been given, taking care of the vegetarian food lovers.

The spices and other ingredients are easily available and all the recipes are simple to follow. Each recipe is detailed and there are tips which make cooking fun.

Surprise your loved ones with the colours, aroma and flavours of Hyderabad.

Nita Mehta

C O N T

E N T S

Rice Dishes 58

Breads 75

Achaar & Chutney 81

Desserts 91

SNACKS

Mirch ke Bhutte

Juicy corn kernels cooked with green chillies. If you like it less spicy, deseed some of the chillies before grinding it to a paste.

Serves 3-4

1¾ cups corn, fresh or frozen

8-10 green chillies - grind with ¼ tsp salt in mixer

2 tbsp oil, 1 tsp salt

1. Heat oil in a *kadhai*. Add green chilli paste and corn together and cook for 5 minutes on medium flame.
2. Add 3-4 tbsp water and stir on low heat for 3-4 minutes. Serve hot.

Hare Boote ke Samose

Patties stuffed with a lemony mixture of fresh green grams.

Makes 20-24

DOUGH

3 cups flour (*maida*)

6-7 tbsp oil

1 tsp salt

FILLING

500 gm fresh tender green gram (*chholia*) - roughly grind in a mixer

1 tsp salt or to taste

75-100 gm green chillies, grind in mixer with 2 tsp oil

3-4 tbsp oil

5-6 tbsp fresh lemon juice

oil for deep frying

1. Put flour and salt in a mixing bowl or a *paraat*. Add 6-7 tbsp oil and rub well with the fingers till you get a crumbly texture. Now start adding water to the flour (*maida*) gradually and bind together. Knead well to make a semi-stiff dough. Cover the dough and keep aside in the fridge for ½ hour.
2. Heat 1 tbsp of oil in a *kadahi*. Add green chilli paste and fry for 1-2 minutes. Add 4 tbsp water and cook for 3-4 minutes. Add the roughly ground green gram and salt mixture and stir fry for 10 minutes on medium flame. Add 4-5 tbsp water if required and cook till the gram is tender and dry. Remove from fire and add lemon juice.
3. Take a small lemon size ball of dough. Roll the dough with a rolling pin (*belan*) very finely into a round disc of about 4½" diameter. Cut the rolled out dough at the centre in two halves. Fold each half to form a cone. Wet the cone edges. Stuff the cone with the gram filling and seal the edges using a little water if required. Repeat the process for the remaining dough and filling.
4. Heat oil for deep frying. Reduce heat and add 5-6 samosas. Fry on low heat, turning sides till the outer maida covering gets cooked and the samosas turn crisp and golden. Serve hot with imli chutney.

Tootak

A baked patty in a cone of semolina, the Tootak is a contribution of the local Hindu Kayastha community.

Makes 10-12

2 cups semolina (*sooji*), 4 tbsp ghee (chilled)
¾ tsp salt, ½ cup milk, approx.

CRUSH SPICES TOGETHER
½ tsp black cumin seeds (*shah jeera*)
seeds of 2 green cardamoms, 1 clove (*laung*)

MINCE FILLING
200 gm mutton mince, 4 tbsp oil
1 large onion - ground to smooth paste
½ tsp ginger paste, 1 tsp garlic paste, ¾ tsp salt, or to taste
¼ tsp turmeric powder, ¾ tsp red chilli powder
¼ cup green coriander (chopped), 1-2 green chillies - finely chopped
2-3 tbsp lemon juice

1. Mix chilled ghee, ground spices and salt with the semolina in a *paraat*, mix well till a ball made with the semolina holds together. Cover and cool in the refrigerator for about half an hour.
2. For filling, heat oil in a kadhai. Add the onion paste, cook on medium flame till golden brown, add ginger and garlic paste, salt, turmeric, red chilli and 4-5 tbsp water to avoid sticking. Cook for 2-3 minutes. Add the mince and stir for 6-8 minutes. Cover and cook till mince is cooked. Uncover and dry if wet.
3. Take out the semolina mixture from the fridge. Add a little milk at a time and knead to make a medium soft dough. Keep aside for 15 minutes.
4. Take a big lemon sized ball of the dough, and shape it into a round ball. Then flatten it somewhat between your palms & with your thumb make a depression in the middle. Press it at the bottom and sides to create a small bowl. Stuff it with about 1 tbsp of mince. Fold the sides and press on top so as to seal the mince. The shape should be flattish at the bottom gentle cone-like in the middle and rounded at the top. Brush with little oil. Make the remaining tootaks also.
5. Preheat oven at 160°C. Place tootaks on a baking tray and bake for 15-20 minutes. Grill for 2-3 minutes to get a nice golden brown top and crisp texture.

Aloo ke Garlay

Fried gramflour balls are pounded and mixed with spicy potatoes to make these savoury balls.

Makes 14-15

GRAM FLOUR BALLS

1 cup gram flour (*besan*), ¼ cup water, approx.

¼ tsp red chilli powder, 1 tsp salt, approx., oil for frying

POTATO MIXTURE

4 large potatoes - boiled, peeled and mashed

2 onions - finely chopped, 1 tsp ginger paste, 1 tsp garlic paste

¼ tsp turmeric (*haldi*) powder, ½ tsp red chilli powder, 1 tsp salt, 4 tbsp oil

¼ cup green coriander chopped, 8-10 mint leaves - chopped

4 green chillies - chopped, 5-6 tbsp lemon juice

COATING BATTER

½ cup refined flour (*maida*), ½ tsp salt

½ cup gram flour (*besan*), a pinch of baking powder, ¾ cup water, approx.

1. Mix gramflour with salt, red chilli powder and water in a *paraat* to make soft dough. Knead well till smooth and soft.
2. Shape dough into small lemon size balls. Deep fry all the gram flour balls, a few at a time, till golden brown, taking care not to over-fry them. Keep aside.
3. For the potato mix, heat 4 tbsp oil in a pan, add onions and fry till light golden. Add ginger, garlic, turmeric, red chilli powder and salt. Cook for a minute and then add the mashed potatoes. Stir well for 2-3 minutes on medium flame. Remove from fire. Mix coriander, mint leaves, green chillies and lemon juice.
4. Pound or crush the fried gram flour balls roughly in a large bowl. Mix the pounded gram flour with the potatoes. Make into balls slightly bigger than the size of a lemon.
5. Mix all the ingredients of the batter, adding enough water to make a medium thin batter of coating consistency.
6. Heat oil in a kadhai, dip the prepared balls into the batter and fry them, a few at a time. Fry till rich golden brown and serve hot.

MAIN
DISHES

Mirchi ka Saalan

Mirchi ka Saalan is whole green chillies in a masala gravy. A popular Hyderabadi dish!

Serves 4-5

250 gm large green chillies - make a slit on one side

4 medium onions - cut each into 4-6 pieces

2 small lemon size balls of tamarind - soak in 1 cup warm water for 15 minutes

1½ tbsp chopped ginger

2 tbsp chopped garlic

1 tbsp coriander seeds (*sabut dhania*), 1 tsp cumin seeds (*jeera*)

3 tbsp sesame seeds, ¼ cup roasted peanuts

1½ tsp poppy seeds, 2" piece kopra - thickly sliced (dry nariyal)

¼ tsp fenugreek seeds, ¼ tsp turmeric powder

1 tsp red chilli powder, 1 tsp jaggery or sugar

a few curry leaves

1 cup oil, 1 tsp salt

1. Mash tamarind. Strain to get tamarind water.
2. Heat 1 tbsp oil on a *tawa*. Add onions and roast the onions for 8-10 minutes till they soften and turn golden-brown. Keep aside.
3. On the same tawa dry-roast together - coriander seeds, sesame seeds, peanuts, cumin seeds, poppy seeds, kopra and the fenugreek seeds till they darken slightly and smell roasted.
4. Grind together the onions, roasted spices, ginger and garlic, salt, turmeric, red chilli powder and jaggery /sugar in a mixer into a fine paste. Add tamarind water to the mixer and again churn till smooth. Keep aside.
5. Heat oil in kadhai, and deep fry green chillies. As soon as the green chillies acquire a few golden-brown spots, remove from the pan and keep aside.
6. Heat 3-4 tbsp oil in a kadhai, add curry leaves to the oil and after a few seconds, add ground paste. Cook for about 5-10 minutes on medium flame.
7. Add the green chillies. Cook over medium heat, stirring occasionally. Add ½ cup water if the gravy appears too thick. Bring to a boil. Cook for another 4-5 minutes on slow flame till the oil comes to the surface.

Nawabi Guchhi

Serves 4

100 gm (½ packet) mushrooms - cut into halves

1 cup shelled peas

3 tbsp ghee

2 tbsp coriander leaves - chopped

½ tsp garam masala, ½ tsp red chilli powder

NAWABI PASTE

2 onions

1" piece ginger

¼ cup cashew nuts

½ tsp black cumin (*shahi jeera*)

½ tsp ordinary cumin (*jeera*)

1 green chilli, 1 dry red chilli

1. Grind the onions and the cashew nuts along with all the other ingredients of the nawabi paste with a little water to a paste.
2. Heat the ghee and fry the nut and onion paste to a rich golden colour, sprinkling a little water now and then to prevent it from burning. Fry till ghee separates.
3. Add the garam masala and chilli powder. Stir for a few seconds.
4. Add ½ cup water. Boil. Add the mushrooms and peas. Bhuno for 4-5 minutes on low flame.
5. Add 1 cup of water and 1 tbsp coriander leaves. Cook covered on low flame, till the vegetables are done.
6. Remove from fire when the vegetables are cooked and the gravy is slightly thick.
7. Serve hot, garnished with fresh coriander leaves.

Achaar ke Aloo

Potatoes in a Pickle Sauce.

Serves 6

700 gm potatoes - boiled and cut into 1" pieces

5 medium onions - grind in mixer to paste

1½ tsp ginger paste, 1½ tsp garlic paste

1½ tsp red chilli powder, ½ tsp turmeric powder (*haldi*)

1 tsp salt or to taste, oil for frying

MIX TOGETHER

¼ cup vinegar, 2 tsp sugar

TEMPERING (*BAGHAAR*)

2 tbsp oil

1 tsp nigella seeds (*kalonji*), ½ tsp mustard seeds (*rai*)

1 tsp cumin seeds (*jeera*), 8 dry whole red chillies

1. Heat oil for frying in a kadhai. Deep-fry potatoes till golden-brown in colour. Keep aside.
2. Heat 8 tbsp oil. Add onions and fry for 8-10 minutes on medium flame till golden brown.
3. Add ginger and garlic and fry for a minute. Add salt, turmeric, red chilli powder. Mix well.
4. Add fried potatoes and mix well gently. Add about ½ cup water and cook on low heat for about 5 minutes till the spices are well-blended and a slight gravy remains.
5. Remove from fire and add sugar and vinegar water. Mix well gently. Transfer to the serving dish.
6. Heat 2 tbsp oil, add the dry whole red chillies, mustard seeds, cumin seeds and last of all, the nigella seeds. When the mustard seeds begin to splutter and the red chillies darken, pour the baghaar over the dish.

Keoti Dal

The word "Keoti" means a mix of lentils. A medley of four lentils. The first three dals are cooked together whereas the channa dal is cooked separately as the cooking time of this dal is more than the others. They are later mixed together and tempered.

Serves 6

¼ cup red gram lentils *(arhar dal)*, ¼ cup red lentils *(masur dal - dhuli)*

¼ cup split and skinned moong *(dhuli moong dal)*

½ cup yellow split gram lentils *(channe ki dal) - soaked in water for 20 minutes*

2 medium onions - thinly sliced

1 tsp ginger paste, 2 tsp garlic paste

1 tsp turmeric powder, 2 green chillies - keep whole

3-4 tbsp lemon juice or one small green mango cut into small slices

4 tbsp oil, 1½ tsp salt, or to taste

TEMPERING (*BAGHAAR*)

½ tsp mustard seeds, ½ tsp cumin seeds, 4 dry whole red chillies

a few curry leaves, 5-6 cloves of garlic - sliced thinly, 4 tbsp ghee/oil

1. Drain the yellow split gram lentils and put in a pressure cooker. Add ½ cup water and pressure cook to give one whistle or till the pressure develops. Keep on low heat for 3-4 minutes. Remove from fire. Keep aside for 4-5 minutes. Drop the pressure by putting under running water. Remove the dal from the cooker and keep aside. The lentils should be almost tender, without getting mushy.
2. Pressure cook all the three lentils together with 2 cups water, salt and turmeric. Remove from fire after the first whistle. Let the pressure drop by itself.
3. Heat oil. Fry the onions till golden brown. Add ginger and garlic. Fry for a minute or so. Then add the boiled lentils and a little water. When the lentils begin to boil, add the separately boiled split gram lentils, green chillies and the juice of lemon or slices of green mango.
4. For tempering, heat *ghee* or oil. Add mustard and cumin seeds, whole red chillies, cloves of garlic and finally the curry leaves. When the mustard splutters and the red chillies darken, pour the baghaar over the lentils. Serve hot.

Baghaare Baingan

A famous Hyderabadi brinjal curry. Roasted onions are combined with mild spices & stuffed in small brinjals. Tamarind & jaggery give this curry a sweet and sour taste.

Serves 4

250 gm brinjals (small round variety)

2 onions - cut each into 4-6 pieces

2 tsp roughly chopped ginger

1 tbsp chopped garlic

1 tsp coriander seeds, 1½ tbsp sesame seeds

3 tbsp roasted peanuts, ½ tsp cumin seeds (*jeera*), 1 tsp poppy seeds (*khus khus*)

1 " square piece kopra (*dry nariyal*), a pinch fenugreek seeds (*methi dana*)

¼ tsp turmeric powder (*haldi*), ½ tsp red chilli powder

½ tsp jaggery (*gur*) or sugar

1 lemon size ball tamarind - soak in 1 cup hot water for 15 minutes, mash and strain

a few curry leaves, ½ cup oil, ½ tsp salt or to taste

1. Wash brinjals. Make cross-slits along the length of the brinjal ensuring that the brinjal is held together at the stem. Keep aside.
2. Roast the onions on a tawa for 8-10 minutes, till they soften a little and turn slightly golden brown.
3. Then dry roast together, on tawa for a minute over medium heat, the coriander seeds, sesame seeds, peanuts, cumin seeds, poppy seeds, kopra and fenugreek seeds till they darken slightly and give out a roasted smell.
4. Grind together the onions, roasted spices, ginger, garlic, salt, turmeric, red chilli powder and jaggery/sugar to a fine paste. Using only about 4-5 tbsp of this paste, stuff the brinjals. Keep stuffed brinjals aside. Add tamarind water to the remaining paste.
5. Heat oil in a pan, add curry leaves and after a few seconds, add the stuffed brinjals. Shake the pan instead of stirring, to brown the brinjals evenly, for about 10 minutes.
6. Add the ground spice paste mixed with tamarind water. Cook covered over medium heat for 5-7 minutes. Add ½ cup water and stir occasionally till brinjals get tender and oil separates. Serve hot.

Khatte Meethe Aloo

Sweet and sour potatoes. Quick and simple to prepare.

Serves 6

500 gm potatoes

1 cup coconut milk, see note

½ tsp mustard seeds (*rai or sarson*)

a few curry leaves

1 tsp black cumin (*shah jeera*)

6 green chillies - grind in mixer to paste

2 tsp grated ginger

½ tsp turmeric powder (*haldi*)

1 tsp salt or to taste

4 green chillies - hand broken into half

2 tsp sugar or to taste

6 tbsp lemon juice, ¼ cup oil

1. Boil the potatoes. Peel and cut potatoes into 1" pieces. Keep aside.
2. Heat oil in a kadhai, add black cumin and mustard seeds. When they crackle, add the curry leaves. Stir.
3. Add the green chilli paste and fry for a minute. Then add the grated ginger, turmeric and salt. Mix well.
4. Add potatoes and mix gently without stirring too much for about 5 minutes.
5. Add the green chillies and the coconut milk, mix well and simmer for 2 minutes.
6. Remove from fire and add lemon juice. Add sugar to taste. Mix lightly. Adjust the sweetness and sourness to your taste.

Note

For coconut milk, grate a fresh coconut, add 1½ cups hot water to it and blend in a mixer. Strain to get coconut milk. Or, you may use ready made coconut milk.

Chowgra

A colourful curry of six different vegetables, creating a range of textures and flavours. Each vegetable is first fried separately and then mixed together and flavoured with aromatic spices.

Serves 6

2 potatoes - cut into ¾" pieces

2 medium carrots - cut into ¼" thick slices

12-15 French beans - cut into 1 ½" pieces

10-12 medium or 1" size florets of cauliflower

2 thin, long brinjals - cut into half lengthwise and then cut diagonally into 1½" pieces

¼ cup frozen or boiled peas, 3 medium size onions - thinly sliced

1 tsp ginger paste, 1 tsp garlic paste

1 tsp salt, ¼ tsp turmeric powder, 1 tsp red chilli powder

1 cup yogurt - whisked till very smooth, oil for frying

GRIND TOGETHER

2 green cardamoms (*illaichi*), 4 cloves (*laung*), 1 bay leaf (*tej patta*)

¼" piece of cinnamon (*dalchini*), ¼ tsp black cumin (*shah jeera*)

1. Heat oil in a kadhai. Deep fry potatoes on low medium heat till golden and almost cooked. Remove from oil. Add cauliflower and fry till light golden, for about 2 minutes. Add brinjals and deep fry till they start changing colour. Add the carrots and fry for just a minute to retain their colour. Similarly fry the beans for just a minute. Set aside.
2. Remove excess oil from the kadhai, leaving about 4 tbsp oil. Heat oil and add onions. Fry for 8-10 minutes till golden brown.
3. Reduce heat. Add ginger and garlic and fry for a minute. Add salt, turmeric and red chilli powder. Sprinkle 2-3 tbsp water and simmer for 2-3 minutes for the spices to blend well.
4. Keeping the heat to a minimum, add the fried vegetables and whisked yogurt. Stir and cook at medium-low heat, till the vegetables are fully cooked. Sprinkle a little water while cooking, if required.
5. Add the ground spices and mix well. Serve hot.

Tamatar Kut

A seasoned tomato curry which is tempered with distinctly Southern spices.

Serves 4-5

1 kg ripe, red tomatoes - roughly chopped

1 tsp ginger paste, 1 tsp garlic paste

¼ tsp fenugreek seeds (*methi daana*), 1 small bunch of curry leaves

1 tsp cumin seeds - roasted and ground (*bhuna jeera*)

3 onions - sliced

1 tsp red chilli powder, ¼ tsp turmeric powder (*haldi*), 1½ tsp salt, or to taste

1 tbsp sesame seeds (*til)* - roasted and coarsely ground

2 tbsp gram flour (besan) - roasted to a light golden brown

5-6 tbsp oil

TEMPERING (*BAGHAAR*)

½ tsp cumin seeds (*jeera*), ½ tsp mustard seeds (*sarson*), ¼ tbsp nigella seeds (*kalonji*)

¼ tsp fenugreek seeds (*methi dana*), 7-8 dry whole red chillies, a few curry leaves

6 tbsp oil

1. Pressure cook the tomatoes with 1½ cups water, ½ tsp each of ginger and garlic, curry leaves, ¼ tsp fenugreek seeds and roasted cumin powder for 4-5 minutes after the pressure forms. Remove from fire and let the pressure drop by itself. Sieve through a strainer to get a fine tomato puree.
2. Heat oil. Fry the onions till golden brown. Add the remaining ginger and garlic and fry for a minute. Add the tomato puree, salt, turmeric, red chilli powder and the roasted and crushed sesame seeds.
3. Blend the roasted gram flour with a little water and add to the tomatoes. Simmer for about 10 minutes over medium heat. Add a little water, if required, to attain a thick soup like consistency.
4. For baghaar, heat oil. Reduce heat. Add the ingredients of the baghaar. When whole red chillies turn brown, add the baghaar to the tomato mixture and cover. Serve hot.

Khatti Dal

Soured lentil curry. The dal is cooked with tomatoes & later again soured with tamarind. The quantity of tamarind is one's own preference. The Hyderabadi baghaar gives it a perky taste.

Serves 4

1 cup red gram lentils (*arhar dal*)

2 tomatoes - chopped finely

a few curry leaves along with stem, ½ tsp grated ginger, 1 tsp crushed garlic

1½ tsp salt or to taste, ¼ tsp turmeric powder, 1 tsp red chilli powder

1 tsp coriander powder

1 lemon size ball tamarind - soaked in ¾ cup hot water for 15 minutes

2-3 green chillies - keep whole, 2-3 tbsp chopped green coriander

TEMPERING (*BAGHAAR*)

½ tsp cumin seeds, 4-5 whole dry red chillies

6-8 cloves of garlic - sliced thinly, 15-20 curry leaves

4 tbsp desi ghee or oil

1. Wash the lentils well. Put in a pressure cooker. Add 3 cups water, tomatoes, sprigs of curry leaves, ginger and garlic. Pressure cook to allow one whistle. Keep on low heat for 5-6 minutes. Remove from fire. Let the pressure drop. Sieve the dal to get a smooth dal.
2. Mash the tamarind and then strain to get tamarind water. Keep aside.
3. Heat the boiled lentils. Add salt, turmeric, chilli powder and coriander powder. Add the tamarind water and cook on slow fire for 5-10 minutes. Add fresh coriander and green chillies.
4. For baghaar, heat *ghee;* add garlic, dry whole red chillies, cumin seeds and curry leaves. When the whole red chillies darken, pour the baghaar over the lentils and cover. Serve hot with plain rice.

Aamras ke Aloo

This mildly sweet and sour potato curry with mango pulp belongs to the khorma family.

Serves 6

500 gm (5) potatoes - boiled and cut into medium-small pieces
½ tsp black cumin (*shah jeera*), 2 green cardamoms (*illaichi*), 2 cloves (*laung*)
3 onions - ground to a paste, ½ tsp ginger paste, ½ tsp garlic paste
1 tsp salt, or to taste, ¼ tsp turmeric powder (*haldi*), 1 tsp red chilli powder
2 tbsp watermelon or musk-melon seeds (*magaz*) - soak in water for 15 minutes and grind to a paste with some water
1 cup yogurt, 2 tbsp fresh cream
a pinch of saffron
½ cup pulp of ripe mangoes
juice of one lemon, or to taste

GRIND TO A POWDER
2 cloves (*laung*), seeds of 2 green cardamoms (*illaichi*)
½ tsp black cumin (*shah jeera*), 1 tsp peppercorns (*sabut kali mirch*)

1. Deep fry potatoes till golden. Keep aside.
2. Mix ground paste of melon seeds with yogurt and whisk well till smooth. Keep aside.
3. Heat 6 tbsp oil. Put in the whole spices - cumin seeds, cloves and cardamom. Wait for a minute.
4. Add the onions and fry till golden brown. Reduce heat. Add ginger, garlic, salt, turmeric and red chilli powder and stir for a few seconds.
5. Add yogurt mixed with ground melon seeds. Stir and cook for 2-3 minutes over medium heat, uncovered. Add about ½ cup water if required.
6. Add the fried potatoes. Mix well. Add the mango pulp, fresh cream and saffron.
7. Add ground spices. Add lemon juice to taste depending on the sweetness of mango pulp. Cook for a minute or two and remove from the heat. Serve hot.

Tamatar aur Channe ki Dal

Tomato and split lentil curry. The dish is of medium-thin consistency and tastes good with rice.

Serves 4

500 gm tomatoes - chopped roughly

½ cup split gram lentils *(channe ki dal)*

1 onion - thinly sliced

½ tsp ginger paste, 1 tsp garlic paste, ¼ tsp turmeric powder

½ tsp red chilli powder, 1-2 green chillies

a few curry leaves

3 tbsp oil

1 tsp salt, or to taste

1. Wash lentils. Add 1¼ cup water and pressure cook to give 1 whistle and then keep on low heat for 3-4 minutes. Remove from fire and let the pressure drop by itself. Keep aside.
2. Heat oil. Add onions and curry leaves. Fry till golden brown. Add ginger and garlic.
3. Stir for a minute. Add salt, turmeric and red chilli powder. Mix.
4. Add the tomatoes. Cook for 3-4 minutes. Add a little water, boiled lentils and green chillies broken in two pieces. Cook for a few minutes. Serve hot.

Besan ke Nimboo

Lemon-flavoured gram flour dumplings in curry simulate the lemon in looks and also somewhat in taste.

Serves 6-8

GRAM FLOUR BALLS

2 cups gram flour (*besan*)

½ cup clarified butter (*ghee*)

½ tsp red chilli powder, ½ tsp ginger, ½ tsp garlic paste

3-4 tbsp chopped green coriander, 2 green chillies - chopped, 4 tbsp lemon juice

½ tsp baking soda, oil for frying, 1 tsp salt

THIN COATING BATTER

2 tbsp gramflour, salt and red chilli powder to taste

FOR THE GRAVY

50 gm or 2 lemon size balls of tamarind - soaked in 3½ cups of hot water for 15 minutes

½ tsp ginger paste, ½ tsp garlic paste

¼ tsp turmeric powder (*haldi*)

4 tsp roasted gram flour (reserved from gram flour balls while roasting)

1 tsp sugar, 1 tsp ghee, 1 tsp salt

DRY ROAST TOGETHER ON A TAWA AND GRIND TO A PASTE

2 tsp sesame seeds *(til)*, 2 tsp poppy seeds (*khus khus*)

2 tsp coriander seeds (*sabut dhania*), 2" piece of kopra (*dry nariyal*)

2 tbsp peanuts (*moongphali*)

FOR THE SEASONING

2-3 tbsp oil, ½ tsp cumin seeds (*jeera*), 4 whole dry red chillies, a few curry leaves

1. To prepare gram flour balls, heat ghee in a heavy-bottom pan. Add the gram flour and fry at low heat till the gram flour is golden brown and gives out a roasted fragrance. Reserve 4 tsp of the gram flour to use later for thickening the gravy. Add salt, chilli powder, ginger and garlic paste, coriander, green chillies and baking soda to the roasted gram flour. Also add the lemon juice. Add a little water and knead well to make dough.
2. Take about one tbsp of the gram flour at a time and roll to make round lemon-sized balls.

3. Take 2 tbsp of gram flour. Add salt, red chilli powder and a little water to make a batter of very thin consistency. Now dip the balls into this batter and deep fry to a golden brown. Set aside
4. For the gravy, soak tamarind in about 3 cups water for 15 minutes. Mash and sieve to get tamarind water. Discard the residue.
5. Lightly dry-roast spices together and grind them to a fine paste. Add the ginger and garlic paste salt, turmeric and red chilli powder to the paste and then mix it with the tamarind water. Add 2 cups of water.
6. Heat the tamarind gravy mixture, prepared above, and bring to a boil. Boil for about 5 minutes. To thicken the gravy add 4 tsp of the roasted gram flour mixed in a little water. Stir and cook at low heat, covered, for about 5 to 7 minutes. Add sugar to taste.
7. For the seasoning, heat oil. Put in the whole red chillies and the cumin seeds. When the colour of the red chillies becomes dark brown, add the curry leaves. After a few seconds, pour the baghaar over the curry.
8. Arrange the fried gram flour balls in a serving dish and pour the curry over the balls. Drop one tsp of ghee into the dish. Serve hot.

Tamatar ki Tarkari

A simple curry of tomatoes.

Serves 4-6

1 kg red tomatoes - put in boiling water for 2 minutes, peel and cut into 4 long pieces

2 medium onions - grind in mixer to a paste

½ tsp ginger paste

1 tsp garlic paste

¼ tsp turmeric powder

1 tsp red chilli powder

1 tsp cumin seeds

5 dry red chillies

a few curry leaves

¼ cup oil, 1-1½ tsp salt

1. Heat oil in a kadhai. Add dry red chillies and cumin seeds. Fry till red chillies darken, add the curry leaves, then add the onions and fry for 8-10 minutes on medium flame till golden brown.
2. Add ginger and garlic, salt, turmeric and red chilli powder cook for 1-2 minutes and then add the tomatoes. Cook first on high heat for 2 minutes then reduce heat, cook covered for 5-7 minutes on low heat till the tomatoes are fully cooked and the oil comes to the surface. Serve hot.

RICE
DISHES

Tahiri

A flavourful biryani of several vegetables.

Serves 4-5

1 cup long grain basmati rice

½ cup shelled peas, 2 potatoes - cut into 1" pieces

2 brinjals, cut from middle length wise then slices into 1-1½" pieces

½ medium size cauliflower, cut into 2" pieces, 3 medium onions - sliced thinly

1 tsp ginger paste, 1 tsp garlic paste, 5-6 green chillies - chopped & crushed in mixer

¼ tsp red chilli powder, ½ tsp turmeric powder, 1 tsp salt or to taste

½ tsp caraway seeds (*shah jeera*), 1 bay leaf (*tej patta*), 1" cinnamon stick (*dalchini*)

½ cup yogurt whisk till very smooth, 3-4 tbsp chopped green coriander

4 tbsp chopped mint leaves, 2 tbsp ghee - to dot, 2 tbsp lemon juice

BIRYANI SPICE POWDER (GRIND TOGETHER)

½ tsp black cumin *(shah jeera)*, 4 cloves (*laung*)

2 green cardamoms (*chhoti illaichi*)

1. Boil 8-10 cups of water with 1 tsp salt. Add rice. Boil for 7-8 minutes, checking the grain by pressing between the thumb and finger to see if it is 70% cooked. Strain and keep the parboiled rice aside.
2. Heat oil for frying. Fry all the vegetables till they are more than half-cooked, one variety at a time. Start with peas. Fry for a second and remove from oil. Add potatoes and fry on low medium heat till cooked and golden. Add the cauliflower with stalk side down and fry for 2-3 minutes. Similarly fry the brinjals.
3. Heat 6 tbsp oil. Add all the spices - caraway seeds, bay leaf and cinnamon to the oil. When their shade darkens a little (this takes a few seconds), add the onions and fry till golden. Add the ginger, garlic, salt, ground green chillies, red chilli powder and turmeric and fry a little.
4. Add the vegetables. Mix well. Remove from fire and add the yogurt.
5. Brush the bottom of another heavy-based handi with oil. Spread half the cooked rice. Pour the vegetables to form a layer. Spread the balance rice to cover the vegetables. Dot it with ghee. Sprinkle coriander, mint and chopped green chillies. Squeeze the lemon juice. Sprinkle biryani powder. Cover with foil and keep on a hot tawa. Reduce heat and keep on low heat for 15 minutes. Serve.

Tamatar ke Chaawal

A flaming red tomato rice dish, made so with tomato and red chilli powder.

Serves 4

1 cup raw rice

1 tsp red chilli powder

2 large tomatoes - chopped finely

2 medium tomatoes - cut into 6 pieces

2 green chillies - slit, 2 tbsp lemon juice

4-5 tbsp oil

1½ tsp salt

1. Boil 6-8 cups water with 2 tsp salt. Add washed rice. Cook for 7-8 minutes till rice turns tender but yet firm to bite. Do not overcook you will make it mushy. Strain. Leave in the strainer for 10 minutes for the water to drain off. Spread on a tray and fluff with a fork to let the steam escape. Keep aside.
2. Heat oil. Add the chopped tomatoes. Cook for 4-5 minutes. Add salt, red chilli powder and green chillies.
3. Add the larger pieces of tomatoes and cook for another couple of minutes.
4. Add rice. Mix. Simmer covered till the rice becomes steaming hot. Add lemon juice. Serve hot.

Imli Til ke Chaawal

Rice flavoured with tamarind and sesame seeds.

Serves 3-4

1½ cups uncooked rice

2 lemon size balls (50 gm) tamarind (*imli*) - soaked in 1 cup hot water for 15 minutes

1 large onion - thinly sliced

½ tsp ginger paste

½ tsp garlic paste

¼ tsp turmeric powder (*haldi*)

1 tsp red chilli powder, 1½ tsp salt

3 tbsp sesame seeds - dry roasted on tawa till golden

5 tbsp oil

1. Boil 6-8 cups water with 2 tsp salt. Add washed rice. Cook for 7-8 minutes till rice turns tender but yet firm to bite. Do not over cook. Strain. Leave in the strainer for 10 minutes for the water to drain off. Spread on a tray and fluff with a fork to let the steam escape. Keep aside.
2. Mash the soaked tamarind and sieve to get tamarind water. Discard the residue. Keep aside.
3. Heat oil. Add onions and fry till golden brown.
4. Add ginger, garlic, salt, turmeric and red chilli powder. Stir.
5. Add tamarind water and cook for 2-3 minutes.
6. Reserving half of the sesame seeds for topping, add the remaining half of the sesame seeds to the tamarind and cook for 2-3 minutes.
7. Add rice. Mix well. Cover and keep on low heat for a few minutes. Serve steaming-hot topped with roasted sesame seeds.

Qabooli

A vegetable biryani with split gram lentils. The word qabooli means acceptable or palatable and the rice is definitely delicious.

Serves 8

3 cups long grain rice - soak for 20 minutes

½ cup yellow split gram lentils (*channe ki dal*) - soak for 20 minutes

1 cup yogurt

3 onions - finely sliced, 1 tsp ginger paste, 1 tsp garlic paste

¼ tsp turmeric powder, 1 tsp red chilli powder

juice of 2-3 lemons, a few sprigs of fresh green coriander - chopped

a few fresh green mint leaves - chopped, 4 green chillies - coarsely chopped

¾ cup oil, 2 tbsp ghee, ¼ cup milk

GRIND OR CRUSH TO A POWDER

½" piece cinnamon (*dalchini*), 2-3 green cardamoms (*illaichi*)

½ tsp black cumin seeds (*shah jeera*), ½ tsp peppercorn (*sabut kali mirch*)

1. Boil 1 cup water with ¼ tsp salt and a pinch of turmeric. Add the dal and cook on low heat till tender.
2. Boil a large panful of water (10-12 cups). Add 2 tsp salt to the boiling water. Add rice and stir to mix well. Boil till 80% cooked (soft, yet chewy). Strain. Leave in the strainer for a minute and then spread the parboiled on a tray.
3. Heat oil in a kadhai. Fry the onions till golden brown. Remove half of the onions for later use and set aside. Add ginger and garlic to the onions in the kadhai and stir. Add turmeric and stir.
4. Add yogurt and stir briskly and cook for about 5 minutes. Add the lentils and red chilli powder. Cook for two-three minutes. Check salt and add to taste.
5. Take a heavy-bottomed pan and brush the bottom with a little oil. Spread half of the parboiled rice. Spread the lentils over the rice. Sprinkle the ground spices. Also spread half of the mint, coriander and green chillies and lemon juice. Cover with remaining rice. Sprinkle the milk, the fried onions and balance of the mint, coriander and the lemon juice and dot the rice with ghee.
6. Cover with foil. Keep on a hot tawa for 5 minutes on medium heat. Reduce heat. Let the rice cook on low heat for 10 minutes till the rice is cooked and steaming hot.

Dum Hyderabadi Biryani

Serves 6

RICE

2 cups (250 gm) basmati rice - washed and kept in the strainer for 30 minutes

4-5 green cardamom (*chhoti illaichi*), 2 bay leaves (*tej patta*), 5-6 cloves (*laung*)

3 tsp salt, 1 tbsp lemon juice, 10 cups water

VEGETABLES

2 thin carrots - peeled and cut into round slices, 20 french beans - cut into ¼" pieces

½ of a small cauliflower - cut into small florets

MIX TOGETHER

1½ cups curd, 1 tbsp mint - chopped finely, 1 tbsp coriander - chopped finely

2-3 drops kewra essence or ½ tsp ruh kewra, ½ tsp salt

CRUSHED SPICES TOGETHER

½ tsp black cumin (*shah jeera*), 3-4 blades mace (*javetri*)

seeds of 1 black cardamom (*moti illaichi*), 1 stick of cinnamon (*dalchini*)

OTHER INGREDIENTS

4-5 tbsp melted ghee or oil

8-10 almonds - split into two pieces, 1 tbsp raisins (*kishmish*)

2 large onion - sliced, 3 tsp ginger-garlic paste, 1 tsp red chilli powder, 1½ tsp salt

a few mint leaves (*poodina*), orange and yellow colour

seeds of 4 green cardamoms (*chhoti illaichi*) - crushed to a powder

1 tbsp melted ghee

TO SEAL

aluminium foil and dough

1. Wash rice several times. Strain. Let it be in the strainer for 30 minutes. (Do not soak). Boil 10 cups water with all ingredients given under rice - chhoti illaichi, laung, tej patta, salt and lemon juice. When the water boils, throw in the rice. Stir. Boil just for 4-5 minutes so that the rice is a little chewy and not fully soft.
2. Remove from fire. If you find the grains too hard, let them be in hot water for 2 minutes. Strain in a big steel strainer or a colander. Run a fork frequently in the rice to separate the grains of rice. Now spread rice in a big tray on a cloth. Keep under the fan for 10 minutes. Remove whole spices from the cooked rice.

3. Heat ghee or oil. Add almonds and kishmish. Stir for a few seconds. Remove from oil and keep aside for topping. Add onions and stir till rich brown. Remove half onion and keep aside for garnish. Reduce heat. Add crushed spices, ginger-garlic paste, chilli powder and salt. Mix.

4. Add vegetables and stir for 2 minutes. Reduce heat. Add ½ of the curd mixture leaving some to put on rice later on. Stir to mix. Cook, stirring on low heat till the vegetables are just done or crisp-tender. Do not over cook. After the vegetables are done, a little masala, about ¼ cup should remain (semi dry). If the vegetables turn too dry, add ¼ cup water. Boil. Remove from fire.

5. To assemble the biryani, take a handi or a baking dish. Grease it. Spread 1/3 of the rice in the dish. Spoon some curd on the rice. Sprinkle yellow colour on half of the rice & orange colour on the other half of the rice.

6. Spread half of the vegetables over the rice. Put ½ the rice on the vegetables. Spoon ½ of the curd mix on the rice. Sprinkle colours. Do not mix.
7. Repeat vegetable layer using all the vegetable.
8. Spread remaining rice. Spoon curd on it. Sprinkle colours. Do not mix.
9. Sprinkle illaichi powder and 1 tbsp of melted ghee over the rice. Put a few mint leaves on the rice.
10. Sprinkle browned onions, almonds and kishmish. Cover with foil.
11. Take a big ball of atta dough, roll in into a long strip.
12. Cover the handi with a foil nicely, pressing the edges well. Seal the end of the handi by pressing the dough strip on the foil, sticking it with the handi.
13. Keep in the oven, if using a glass dish, for 'dum' at 150°C for 30 minutes or keep on a tawa, if using a metal handi, on very low heat for 15-20 minutes.

BREADS

Bakharkhani Roti

An exquisitely rich bread which owes its creation to Governor of pre-independence Bengal - Nawab Bakhar Khan.

Serves 6-8

4 cups flour (*maida*)

100 gm clarified butter (*ghee*)

1 tsp salt, 1 tsp baking powder

2 tbsp poppy or nigella seeds for topping, 4 tbsp melted ghee for brushing

MIX TOGETHER

1¼ cups milk, approx.

3 tbsp sugar

4 tbsp screwpine flower (*kewra*) water

SOAK IN WARM WATER FOR 10 MINUTES

10-15 almonds - blanched and sliced thinly

10-15 raisins (*kishmish*)

1 tbsp sunflower seeds (*chironji*)

1. Add salt, baking powder and ghee to the flour. Mix till it becomes crumbly.
2. Mix milk with 3 tbsp sugar and kewra water. Add to the flour gradually and knead to make a medium soft dough.
3. Drain the soaked raisins, almonds and sunflower seeds. Add to dough and mix well. Cover and set aside for 2 hours.
4. Divide the dough into 8 equal portions. Take one portion and roll it into a ball. Dust lightly with flour. On a flat surface roll it out to a thin large disc. Brush the surface with ghee and sprinkle with a little dry flour, fold one third of the disc from one side. Now fold the disc from the other side over the portion folded earlier. Sprinkle some dry flour. Now fold a portion from one side and then the other to make a layered square. Dust it tightly with flour and roll it out to a 6" square. Sprinkle a few poppy or nigella seeds and press them in firmly with a rolling pin (*belan*).
5. Place the uncooked rotis on a greased tray and bake in a pre-heated oven at 160°C for about 12-15 minutes. If you like it crisper grill for 3-4 minutes further till golden brown. Brush with ghee. Serve hot.

Sheermal

A rich bread made with milk and fragrant kewra water.

Makes 12

4 cups whole wheat flour (*atta*)

1¼ cups milk, approx.

6 tbsp desi ghee or white butter

1 tsp salt

2 tbsp sugar

2 tsp dry yeast

4 tbsp screwpine flower water (*kewra water*)

1. Warm 1¼ cups milk. Do not boil, just make it slightly warm. Dissolve sugar and yeast in warm milk. Add screwpine flower water. Cover and keep aside.
2. Add salt and ghee to flour and mix till it gets crumbly. Knead with milk to make medium soft dough. Cover with a damp cloth and set aside for 2-3 hours.
3. Divide the dough in 12 equal portions. Take one portion and roll into a ball. Dust with flour and roll out to a slightly thick round of about 6" diameter. Prick with a fork all over, leaving a margin of one inch on the sides.
4. Place the sheermal on a pre-heated tawa and cook it first on one side and then the other, until both sides are a rich golden brown. Alternatively, pre-heat oven to 350°F/180°C, place the sheermals on a greased tray and bake for about 15 minutes or till rich golden brown and cooked on both sides.

ACHAAR
&
CHUTNEY

Tamatar ki Chutney

Tomato chutney spiked with green chillies. Remember to slit the green chillies before putting in oil or they might burst open.

Serves 8-10

1 kg tomatoes - chopped

1 tsp salt

50 gm green chillies - slit

4 tbsp sesame seeds and 2 tbsp cumin seeds

½ cup oil

FOR BAGHAAR

6 whole red chillies

½ tsp mustard seeds

½ tsp cumin seeds

a few curry leaves

3-4 tbsp oil

1. Dry roast sesame seeds till light golden. Remove from pan. Roast cumin till brown. Grind both seeds together to a powder. Keep aside.
2. Wash and slit the green chillies. Pat dry the chillies. Heat oil and lightly fry the green chillies. Remove from oil and grind to a paste.
3. Heat oil again. Add tomatoes and salt and cook till you get the consistency of tomato puree. Add the ground chillies and the ground cumin and sesame seeds. Mix and cook over low heat till the water dries up and the oil comes to the surface. Transfer to a bowl.
4. Heat about 3-4 tbsp oil for baghaar. When hot add the whole red chillies, cumin and mustard seeds. When the chillies turn a shade darker and the mustard seeds begin to splutter, add the curry leaves and after a few seconds pour the baghaar over the chutney.

Lal Mirch aur Adrak ki Chutney

A delicious sweet and sour ginger-red chilli chutney which is also a digestive.

Makes 1 bowl

60 gm ginger - cut into ½" juliennes (¾ cup)
60 gm jaggery - grated (¼ cup)
125 gm tamarind - soaked in 1 cup water
25 gm (¾ cup) whole, dry, red chillies
½ cup oil, ½ tsp salt, or to taste

FOR BAGHAAR
½ tsp split white lentils without skin (*urad dal - dhuli)*
½ tsp split gram lentils (*channa dal)*
½ tsp sesame seeds (*til*)
a few curry leaves

1. Mash the soaked tamarind and take out the pulp.
2. Heat ½ cup oil. Add whole dry red chillies and fry for a minute till they darken.
3. Grind together the fried chillies, tamarind and jaggery to a paste. Add salt. Keep aside.
4. In the same oil, fry the ginger till golden. Remove from oil and add to the tamarind-ginger paste.
5. For the baghaar, reheat the remaining oil, add both the dals. When the colour of the dals darkens a little, add the til and curry leaves. After a few seconds, pour the baghaar over the ginger-tamarind mixture. Transfer to a clean, dry, air-tight jar when cool.

Til ki Chutney

A sesame seed chutney with a south Indian tempering of red chillies and curry leaves.

Makes 1 bowl

½ cup sesame seeds (*til*)

2 rounded tsp tamarind - soaked in 1¼ cups hot water for 15 minutes

4 green chillies

6 large cloves garlic - chopped (4 tbsp)

1 tsp salt or to taste

TEMPERING (*BAGHAAR*)

1-2 dry whole red chillies

½ tsp mustard seeds

½ tsp cumin seeds

10-15 curry leaves

1 tbsp oil

1. Dry roast the sesame seeds on a *tawa* or a skillet till golden. Remove. Roast the green chillies directly on gas or live charcoal till parts of green chillies turn blackish.
2. Mash the soaked tamarind. Strain the tamarind to get pulp.
3. Grind together the roasted sesame seeds, the green chillies and garlic.
4. Add salt and tamarind pulp to the mixer and blend again. Transfer to a serving dish.
5. Heat oil for tempering. Add mustard and cumin seeds. When the seeds begin to pop and the red chillies begin to darken, add the curry leaves. Mix well and pour it over the chutney.

Aloo Hari Mirch ka Achaar

A spicy pickle of potatoes and green chillies.

Makes 1 small jar

4 large (500 gm) potatoes

150 gm green chillies

2 tsp salt, 2 tsp red chilli powder, ½ tsp turmeric (*haldi*) powder,

1 tsp coriander (*dhania*) powder, 2 tsp cumin (*jeera*) powder

3 tbsp sugar, 1 cup white vinegar

1 cup oil

BAGHAAR

1 tsp cumin seeds (*jeera*), 1 tsp mustard seeds (*rai*)

½ tsp nigella seeds (*kalonji*), ½ tsp fenugreek seeds (*methi dana*)

1 tsp ginger paste, 1 tsp garlic paste

1. Boil the potatoes. Peel the skin and cut them into 1" pieces. Wash the chillies. Leave a little stem with the chillies. Slit the chillies on one side, keeping them whole.
2. Heat 1 cup oil and fry the potatoes till golden. Set aside in a bowl.
3. Fry the green chillies till they wilt just a little and change colour slightly. Remove from oil immediately and add to the fried potatoes.
4. Add salt, chilli powder, turmeric, cumin and coriander powder, sugar and the vinegar to the potatoes and the chillies.
5. Reheat the oil in which potatoes and green chillies were fried. Add cumin and mustard seeds. When the mustard begins to pop, add the nigella and fenugreek seeds and a few seconds later ginger and garlic. Fry for a minute or so. Remove from heat and allow to cool.
6. When cool, add it to the potatoes and green chillies. Transfer the pickle to a dry, clean and air-tight jar.

DESSERTS

Khajoor ka Halwa

A halwa of dates with lentils. An unusual dessert inspired from Arabia.

Serves 6-8

½ kg dates

1½ cups split gram lentils (*channe ki dal*)

1½ kg milk

1½ cups clarified butter (*ghee*)

4 tbsp screwpine flower water (*kewra*)

10-15 almonds - blanched, peeled and cut into thin slices

a few pistachios

seeds of 4-5 green cardamoms - crushed

¼ cup sugar, or to taste

1. Wash the gram lentils and put in a kadhai. Add milk and bring to a boil. Boil on low medium heat for about 20 minutes till the lentils are tender and liquids dry up. Remove from fire and let them cool. Grind the lentils to a paste.
2. Wash and deseed dates. Boil in ¼ cup water for 5-6 minutes. Remove from fire and let it cool. Mash the dates with your hands.
3. Mix dates with lentil paste.
4. Heat ghee in a clean heavy bottom kadhai. Add the dates and lentil mixture and fry well. Then add sugar and cook for another few minutes.
5. Add screwpine flower water and crushed cardamoms. Decorate with almonds and pistachio. Serve.

Double ka Meetha

This bread pudding is a Hyderabadi variety of the Shahi Tukri of North India. The name comes from the word double roti, which is the Indian name for bread.

Serves 15-20

10 slices of fresh white bread - remove crust and cut each into half diagonally

½ kg milk

½ cup cream

1 cup sugar, ½ cup water

a pinch of saffron (*kesar*) - soaked in 2 tbsp rose water

¾ cup clarified butter (*ghee*)

12-15 almonds - blanched and sliced

15 pistachio - sliced

a few sheets of silver leaves (*chandi ke warq*), optional

1. Boil milk. Reduce heat. Cook on medium heat for 10-15 minutes till the consistency is reduced to almost half. Add cream and cook for a minute. Keep aside.
2. Boil sugar in ½ cup water and make syrup. Keep aside to cool. Mix saffron soaked in rose water to sugar syrup.
3. Heat ghee in a pan. Shallow fry the bread slices till light golden on both sides.
4. Brush a baking tray with ghee. Place the bread slices in the tray and soak each slice of bread with about a tbsp of flavoured sugar syrup.
5. Now pour creamy milk on the bread slices. Sprinkle almond and pistachio. Allow the bread to soak in the liquids. Bake in pre-heated oven at 180°C for 15-20 minutes till the liquids almost dry up. Decorate with silver leaves.

Makhane ki Kheer

A dessert of lotus seeds.

Serves 8-10

2 kg milk, 100 gm lotus seeds (*makhane*) - roast for 1-2 minutes in a pan
¾ cup sugar or to taste, ½ tsp green cardamom (*illaichi)* powder
2-3 tbsp screwpine flower (*kewra water)*, 1 tbsp chopped green pista

1. Roast the lotus seeds till they start to change colour. Let them cool. Crush half of them, leaving the other half whole.
2. Boil milk. When the milk starts to boil, add the lotus seeds and cook in milk at medium heat, stirring every now and then. Cook till the lotus seeds are cooked and the consistency of the milk reduced by one third.
3. Add sugar and sprinkle crushed cardamom. Cook further for a couple of minutes. Remove from heat.
4. Add kewra water. Transfer to a serving dish. Decorate with silver leaves and chopped pista.

Khubani ka Meetha

Pulp of apricot with cream. Traditionally the light brown apricots with the seed are used. The kernel of the seed is used as the garnish for the dessert. Here we have used the orange, seedless variety of apricots to make the pulp and garnished with blanched and slivered almonds.

Serves 8-10

½ kg dried apricot (*khubani*)

¾ cup (150 gm) sugar, or to taste, 250 gm fresh cream

GARNISH

almonds

1. Soak apricots overnight with ¼ cup sugar in 2 cups water to cover them.
2. Next morning, boil apricots in the same water till tender. Remove seeds if present.
3. Sieve till only the fibre remains in the strainer.
4. Add a little water, the remaining sugar and cook till you get the consistency of custard. Garnish the dish with almonds. Serve with fresh cream.

Glossary of Names/Terms

HINDI OR ENGLISH NAMES as used in India	USED IN USA/UK/OTHER COUNTRIES
Baingan	Eggplant, aubergine
Bhutta	Corn
Capsicum	Bell peppers
Chhoti Illaichi	Green cardamom
Chilli powder	Red chilli powder, Cayenne pepper
Cornflour	Cornstarch
Dalchini	Cinnamon
French beans	Green beans
Gobhi	Cauliflower
Hara Dhania	Cilantro/fresh or green coriander leaves
Hari Gobhi	Broccoli
Hari Mirch	Green hot peppers, green chillies
Imli	Tamarind
Jeera	Cumin seeds
Saunf	Fennel
Sela Chaawal	Parboiled rice, which when cooked is not sticky at all
Seviyaan	Vermicelli
Soda-bi-carb	Baking soda
Til	Sesame seeds
Toned Milk	Milk with 1% fat content
Yellow Capsicum	Yellow bell peppers

INTERNATIONAL CONVERSION GUIDE

These are not exact equivalents; they've been rounded-off to make measuring easier.

WEIGHTS & MEASURES

METRIC	*IMPERIAL*
15 g	½ oz
30 g	1 oz
60 g	2 oz
90 g	3 oz
125 g	4 oz (¼ lb)
155 g	5 oz
185 g	6 oz
220 g	7 oz
250 g	8 oz (½ lb)
280 g	9 oz
315 g	10 oz
345 g	11 oz
375 g	12 oz (¾ lb)
410 g	13 oz
440 g	14 oz
470 g	15 oz
500 g	16 oz (1 lb)
750 g	24 oz (1½ lb)
1 kg	30 oz (2 lb)

LIQUID MEASURES

METRIC	*IMPERIAL*
30 ml	1 fluid oz
60 ml	2 fluid oz
100 ml	3 fluid oz
125 ml	4 fluid oz
150 ml	5 fluid oz (¼ pint/1 gill)
190 ml	6 fluid oz
250 ml	8 fluid oz
300 ml	10 fluid oz (½ pint)
500 ml	16 fluid oz
600 ml	20 fluid oz (1 pint)
1000 ml	1¾ pints

CUPS & SPOON MEASURES

METRIC	*IMPERIAL*
1 ml	¼ tsp
2 ml	½ tsp
5 ml	1 tsp
15 ml	1 tbsp
60 ml	¼ cup
125 ml	½ cup
250 ml	1 cup

HELPFUL MEASURES

METRIC	*IMPERIAL*
3 mm	1/8 in
6 mm	¼ in
1 cm	½ in
2 cm	¾ in
2.5 cm	1 in
5 cm	2 in
6 cm	2½ in
8 cm	3 in
10 cm	4 in
13 cm	5 in
15 cm	6 in
18 cm	7 in
20 cm	8 in
23 cm	9 in
25 cm	10 in
28 cm	11 in
30 cm	12 in (1ft)

BEST SELLERS BY 

101 Paneer Recipes

101 Vegetarian Recipes

SPECIAL Vegetarian Recipes

Cakes & Cake Decorations

DIABETES Cookbook

Burgers &
Sandwiches

Burgers & Sandwiches

Vegetarian MUGHLAI

CHOCOLATE Cookbook